MW00933757

The 30 Day Romance Novel Workbook

Write a Novel in a Month with the Plot-As-You-Write System

Lynn Johnston

The 30 Day Romance Novel Workbook
2014, 2016 Copyright Lynn Johnston

Open Clearing Press

ISBN-13: 978-1539754817
ISBN-10: 1539754812

This book was originally published under the title *The 30 Day Novel Success Journal for Romance.*

Table of Contents

If you don't go after
what you want,
you'll never have it.

If you don't ask,
the answer is always no.

If you don't step forward,
you're always in the same place.

—Nora Roberts

Introduction

Every year, hundreds of thousands of writers commit to writing 50,000 words or more in the caffeine- and comfort food-fueled endurance test that is National Novel Writing Month (NaNoWriMo).

They sacrifice many of the little comforts that make life easier—television, dinner out with friends, video games, even sleep—so they can hit their daily word count goal.

For 30 days, they become obsessed with one thing: finishing a novel.

Why would anyone put themselves through this kind of ordeal?

- **Because they want to finish.** The more slowly you write, the more likely it is that you'll get bored with this story or lose momentum and get distracted by another great idea.

- **Because they know that inspiration strikes more often when you're writing.** Many aspiring writers make the mistake of only writing when they feel inspired. Experienced authors know that the more deeply you're engaged in a story, the faster the ideas flow. Daily writing sessions keep your subconscious focused on your story so that you're working on it even when you're not writing.

- **Because writing quickly helps you resist the urge to stop and edit.** Editing a novel requires a big-picture perspective on your story. But your perspective on the story is limited while you're writing it, because you don't know what cool ideas your muse is going to hand you three chapters from now. Any editing you do before the rough draft is complete is liable to be flawed, which means you're wasting your time and possibly introducing new problems that you'll have to fix later.

- **Because they know that you can edit anything but a blank page.** Editing can turn a terrible scene into a not-so-bad scene, and a hey-this-has-potential scene into a wow-I-can't-believe-I-wrote-this scene. But you have to get the story down on paper (or flash drive) before you can start working with it.

- **Because they know they can do anything for 30 days.** An ambitious project like writing a novel requires sacrifices—giving up television, noodling on Facebook, hanging out with friends and other fun activities. It's much easier to sacrifice your free time for a worthy project when you know that you're not giving up the fun stuff forever—it's just 30 days.

- **Because they love the adrenaline rush of spending a month on the roller coaster of active creation.** A writing marathon like NaNoWriMo is a great excuse to let your creativity cut loose, to make a heroic effort and have something tangible to show for it at the end. This 30-day program gives you a doable goal, a motivating deadline, and a clear path to completion.

Preparing Yourself

You can increase your chances of successfully completing your rough draft with some simple preparation. This section will help you to ready yourself mentally, to arrange your environment so it supports your creativity, and to plan your project.

Do I Have to Write a Novel?

If you're a new writer and the idea of writing a whole novel seems overwhelming, you can use this program to write the first act of your novel (and then repeat as needed to write the rest, one section at a time).

It's also fine to use this program to write a novella or a short story. If your story is less than 30,000 words, you'll need to adapt the Before You Write prompts accordingly. Or several short stories.

The important thing is that you set a goal that feels exciting to you, and stick to the program for the full 30 days.

Establishing Your Writing Routine

Let's look at your calendar for the 30 day period you've chosen to write your novel.

When will you be able to write? Will you set aside time every day to write (which is the NaNoWriMo recommendation) or will you reserve larger blocks of time on specific days?

It's tempting to treat yourself like a writing machine when coming up with a schedule, but don't forget to give yourself breaks. Numerous studies have shown that, in order to maintain mental focus and produce high-quality creative work, short rest breaks are necessary.

One of the more common suggestions is 50 minutes of mental work followed by 10 minutes away from the computer to stretch out the kinks, get a glass of water, or even meditate. You may or may not find it helpful to spread your writing sessions throughout the day—an hour in the morning, an hour in the evening.

And don't think of this schedule as set in stone, especially if you aren't already in the habit of writing every day. Feel free to experiment until you've discovered the writing routine that works for you.

Does It Have to Be 30 Days in a Row?

No, it doesn't *have* to be 30 days in a row. If, for example, your work schedule is such that you can only find time to write every other day, or Monday through Friday, or something like that, that's fine. Just realize that the more time between writing sessions, the easier it is to lose momentum. By skipping days, you're giving your subconscious a chance to refocus on other projects, which takes you out of the flow of your story.

One way of keeping momentum if you have to skip a day of

writing is to read what you've already written or review the outline of your story on your off-days. Even five minutes of staying in touch with your story when you can't write keeps your subconscious focused on the story, making it easier to jump back into the writing later.

Freeing Up Time to Write

Which of your usual activities will you reduce or eliminate for the next 30 days so you'll have more time to write?

What do you need to do to feel good about giving up these activities?

TiVo favorite shows? Schedule social time after your novel is completed to catch up with friends? Arrange a weekend hiking trip with your sweetie to thank them for supporting your 30-day writing spree?

Now that you've established your writing schedule, get out your calendar and block off the times you're going to write. If you're using an electronic calendar (like Outlook or Gmail), you can set each event up to send you an email reminder or cause a reminder to pop-up on your computer.

Setting Goals

Let's start by setting your goal for the month:

I am going to write *(fill in your project's working title below)*

I will start writing by _____ *(start date),* **and I will finish by** _____ *(end date).*

Daily Word Count

In order to write a 50,000 word novel in 30 days, you must write 1666 words each day.

If you're writing for publication and you've researched your market, you know that publishers consider 50,000 words to be a long novella. Most expect novels be somewhere between 60,000 and 90,000 words long. So you may need to write between 2000 and 3000 words each day, or plan to do more than one 30-day marathon.

If you're new to writing and want to cut your teeth on a shorter project, short stories run 500-10,000 words and novellas run 10,000-60,000. (These are approximate; ranges vary by publisher.)

So, how do you choose the right length for your story?

If you're writing in a specific genre and your goal is to get traditionally published, check out the websites of 2-3 publishers who you might submit to. What do their submission guidelines say?

If you're planning to self-publish, length is up to you. The cost for producing an ebook is the same regardless of length. Print-on-demand services like CreateSpace or Lulu allow you to produce books in a variety of lengths, but the cost of production goes up as the number of pages goes up.

My novel will be _____ words long.

I will write this novel in _____ writing sessions.

Count the actual number of sessions you've set aside if you're deviating from the "write every day for 30 days" formula.

Divide your total word count by the number of days you will write. This number is your daily word count goal.

I will write _____ words each day.

Weekly Word Count

I recommend also having a weekly word count goal. Why? Because it's inevitable that you will have high days and low days. If you don't hit your daily word count goal one day, you won't get discouraged if you make up for it the next day and hit your weekly goal.

I will write _____ words each week.

What If My Word Count Is Off?

It happens. You start writing and realize that you can tell your story well in fewer words than you estimated. Or inspiration strikes and you find yourself adding a subplot that increases your word count by 10,000.

Or maybe it's not the story, maybe it's your style that's caused you to misjudge your word count. Maybe you tend to write skeletal rough drafts and layer in details during edits. (That's me—my stories often come in at 75% of my target word count. I go back and expand on character emotions, add body language and turning lots of telling into showing when I edit.)

Or maybe you're one of those writers who's wordy in the rough draft, but when you edit, you ruthlessly prune your prose.

Either way, it's okay. If you don't know now what kind of writer you are, you'll find out over the next 30 days. Just keep going, and if you need to adjust your daily word count goal, do so.

Staying Motivated

Let's take a moment to focus on your personal reasons for writing this story. Is it a lifelong dream to get published? Is there some message you'd like to share with others? Is this story arising from an experience you've had that you'd like to explore more deeply?

I want to write this story because

Let's also look at your reasons for giving yourself a 30-day deadline. Does the idea of working with a group of other writers, NaNoWriMo-style, give you a boost of motivation? Are you stalled on this novel and hoping that a deadline will help you build momentum? Are you curious to see if you can do it? Or afraid that if you don't do it soon, you won't ever get started?

I want to write this story in 30 days because

Now I'd like you to close your eyes and image how you're going to feel on Day 30 when you type the last sentence of your novel. Do you feel elated? Do you want to tell someone? Describe how you think it will feel to be able to say, "I wrote a novel!"

When your spirits flag and you're tempted to skip a day of writing, come back to this section and reconnect with your reasons for writing your novel.

Rewarding Yourself

To keep your motivation high, I suggest that you reward yourself for progress.

I try to give myself a small reward for every day that I meet or exceed my word count goal, and a big reward for hitting my total word count goal at the end of the 30 days.

For the sake of your health, you might not want to use food as a reward. Throwing your body out of whack with too many high-sugar or high-carb treats is not only bad for the waistline, but it can affect your productivity: your brain needs a steady supply of blood sugar to run efficiently. Blood sugar spikes and crashes can leave you feeling you moody, tired, and unfocused—not the best state of mind for creative work.

One of the best places to start when looking for rewards is that list of things you decided to give up for 30 days. TV shows, video games, reading for fun, chatting with friends online—make yourself earn the right to spend 30 minutes goofing around by meeting your daily word count goal.

If you decide to buy yourself rewards, just make sure they fit into your monthly budget.

Fighting Off Fatigue

Unless you are already in the habit of turning out a couple thousand words per day, you are going to experience periods of mental and emotional fatigue at least once during your thirty day marathon. This is because you are pushing yourself to think hard about your story while also following your characters on an emotional rollercoaster—necessary in order to create an emotionally-compelling story.

If you're planning to write straight through without breaks, you'll need to take extra care of yourself physically so you'll have the stamina to make it to Day 30. Good food, good sleep, and most importantly, short rejuvenation breaks throughout the day (like a brief meditation, or a brisk walk, or anything else that refreshes you). I like to use brainwave entrainment for a quick mental "reset", and I find that short breathing exercises can help me recharge when I don't feel like I can afford to take a day off from writing.

Tracking Your Progress

It can be highly motivating to track your progress visually. If you've got a chart (like the one in this book) where you mark off each successful day, this visual representation of your progress can stoke the fires of motivation. Other ways to keep track of your progress visually:

- Get a glass jar and drop in a marble every time you write 250 words (the equivalent of a properly-formatted manuscript page).
- Print out each day's writing and keep the ever-growing stack of paper on a corner of your desk.
- Thumbtack a piece of paper on the wall next to your desk and keep a prison-style tally of writing days.

It doesn't matter what system you use, as long as you do something to track your progress in a way that you can see it at all times.

Don't forget to reward yourself when the novel is written, either. It doesn't have to be expensive, as long as it's meaningful. I recommend celebrating with a supportive friend, family member or fellow writer.

In addition to rewarding yourself and tracking your progress, I recommend buddying up with another writer, if possible. Check in with each other every day, by phone, email, or chat, to report progress. It is important that these check-ins be positive—no criticism or guilt trips allowed. If one of you doesn't hit a daily goal, the other should only offer emotional support and encouragment, and ask what the plan is for the next day.

Another way to use accountability to stay motivated is to post your progress somewhere publicly. You may already belong to a writing group where this is an option. During NaNoWriMo, the forums there are a great way to meet other writers.

My only caution is that you not share your progress anywhere that you might receive discouragement for it. So if your Facebook circle includes your ubercriticial brother-in-law, that might not be the right place to post updates on your novel unless you're sure that negative comments won't discourage you.

Drawing on Past Experience

If you have written a novel before:
What obstacles did you face, and how did you overcome them?

What did you learn about novel writing?

What positive influences or conditions helped you succeed in writing that novel?

Do you still have access to each of those positive influences or conditions? If not, is there anything you can do to recreate them?

If you've started a novel that you've not yet finished:

Why did you stop? How do you think you might deal with those obstacles if you encounter them again?

If you've never tried to write a novel before:

What other types of writing have you succeeded at in your life?

What obstacles did you face, and how did you overcome them?

What obstacles do you anticipate in writing a novel?

What possible solutions might you try for each obstacle?

Physical Preparation

Where do you plan to write your novel? Will you be relying on visits to a cafe or library? Do you have a space at home where you can write uninterrupted? Will you be writing on the train during your daily commute or on your lunch hour?

Wherever you're going to work on your novel, take a few minutes to evaluate it in terms of physical comfort. Could you make the chair more comfortable with a lumbar pillow or ease the strain on your wrists with a wrist rest? Will you need to wear a sweater or add a small fan to adjust the temperature? Would earplugs (easy to find at the drugstore) or music improve your concentration? Is there an unpleasant smell that you might want to eliminate with an air filter or aromatherapy candle?

Also, what equipment will you need to store here? Extra batteries? A pad of paper and a pen for sketching maps of your locations? A printed thesaurus to eliminate the temptation to connect to the internet?

Will you need to talk with anyone in order to protect your writing time? Ask your husband to watch the kids after dinner? Put a lock on the door so your roommates won't barge in and interrupt your train of thought?

Will you do all your writing at a café or some other place

where you can't store your stuff? Identify everything you'll need and pack it in a bag to take with you. If you're alternating between writing outside the home and writing at home, make sure you always put your writing materials back in the bag at the end of the at-home sessions, so you don't have to worry about forgetting a crucial item when you head to the café.

Do you have a small notebook that you can carry with you to jot down ideas when you're not writing?

Finally, I recommend that you choose a book that you will use as a model for when you get stuck—preferably a book in the same genre that you're writing. Keep this book in your writing area or with your writing supplies.

How do you use this model book to get yourself unstuck?

Let's say you're writing a fight scene, and you're not sure how to describe your hero's fistfight with your villain. Find a fight scene in your model book and analyze how the author handled the fight.

Did they use a lot of big words and long sentences, or is the fight scene tersely worded? How much dialogue is there? How long is it? How much of the fight is described blow-by-blow and how much is summarized? How much attention is placed on the hero and how much is placed on the villain?

Often, gaining a deeper understanding of how another author has made decisions in a similar scene will give you ideas about how to approach your own.

Getting Into the Right Mindset

One of the biggest dangers in attempting to write a novel at this pace is burnout.

Psychological studies have shown that we have a certain amount of creative energy each day, and that this energy is depleted as we use it to make decisions—whether those decisions are creative or not.

This creative energy is linked to physical vitality, so taking good care of your body by eating well, exercising regularly, getting enough sleep and actively managing stress can increase how much creative energy you have available for writing. The better care you take of your body, the less likely you are to burn out before your 30 days is over.

What If I Get Stuck?

The two most common reasons for getting stuck while writing:

1. **You're not clear on some aspect of the story, and you need to spend some time thinking it through at a deeper level.**

Whenever you're not sure what happens next in your story,

take a few minutes to review your characters' goals and motivations, and think about what conflicts they're likely to encounter given the world you've put them in.

Sometimes this is enough to spark your inspiration. But if you still don't know what happens next, here's an exercise I learned from Holly Lisle (a brilliant writing teacher; I highly recommend all of her books and writing workshops—check out her website: hollylisle.com).

Start your scene by writing: "This is the scene where..." and describe what you know about the character's current situation.

Write what the characters might be thinking and feeling after what happened in the last scene, and what those thoughts and feelings make them want to do.

Write what the characters would like to say to each other, why they're holding themselves back, what they'd rather be doing and why they can't do that.

Write about the setting and the dangers that might be lurking in it for the characters.

Freewriting about different aspects of the scene will often trigger the new idea that gets you moving forward again.

2. You're trying to make your writing perfect, and your inner editor is stifling your creative flow.

This one's harder to fix because it feels like stopping to find exactly the right synonym for "walked" is crucial to making the story work.

But here's the thing—stopping to invoke your inner editor blocks the flow of creativity. Who knows how long it'll take you to get back into the flow once you've chosen a better synonym?

Sometimes you won't be able to get back into the flow at all.

The same goes for researching what kind of sandals a centurion would wear, looking up Spanish swear words for your villain to yell, and searching an online map of Chicago for the street where your heroine's favorite bookstore is located.

The pro writer's trick for keeping creative flow going when you're tempted to stop is to put an asterisk by anything you need to go back and research/decide/brainstorm later.

It's better to type Streetname* than to ask your muse to wait half an hour while you play on Google Maps.

It's better to type Thug-A* and Thug-B* than to stop your story to contemplate Russian surnames for your mobster's henchmen.

Get the story down now, and when it's finished, come back and use your word processor's search function to find all those asterisks and fill in the blanks.

If your inner editor is obssessing on word choice rather than story details, here are some techniques for keeping the flow going:

- Turn off your screen so you can't see what you've written.
- Every time you're tempted to polish your prose, say out loud, "We'll fix that later, after the story's done." Then write the next sentence.
- Check out Write or Die (writeordie.com), a writing app that will actually delete words if you stop typing for too long. (Personally, I find this more stressful than motivating, but I know writers who love it.)

Sometimes you'll get a cool new idea as you're writing, and you'll realize that what you wrote earlier doesn't fit with the new direction you're taking the story.

Do not go back and revise.

Instead, make a note of the changes you think you'll need, and push on to the end.

Why shouldn't you stop and revise as soon as you realize that you need to make a change?

Because you might come up with even more cool ideas as you get closer to the finish, and you don't want to waste time revising until you're sure you've got the whole picture.

Preparing Your Story

Experienced writers, you probably already have a collection of story development tools that work for you.

New writers, if you're not sure what you need to know before you can start writing your novel, this section will help you figure that out.

Plotters vs Pantsers

Writers seem to fall across a spectrum between two extremes:

Plotters: these writers figure the story out in great detail before they write a word, and prefer to write from an in-depth outline (which they may rework as new ideas occur).

Plotters are drawn to lists and charts and structured brainstorming exercises where they decide what the story's theme will be and how the protagonist's growth arc will unfold.

Pantsers: These writers start with a character, an image, or a scenario, and figure out the plot as they go. They may or may not identify major plot points up front. They may or may not know how the story ends.

Pantsers are the ones who tend to rhapsodize about characters talking to them or surprising them by doing unexpected things.

In between these two extremes are writers who do varying amounts of pre-writing exercises before they start the actual draft.

Most writers fall somewhere between these two extremes.

If you're closer to the pantser end of the spectrum, I encourage you to skim this section and contemplate some of these questions. Even if you don't take the time to write out answers, just bringing these questions into your awareness will start your subconscious thinking about your story from new perspectives.

The closer you are to the plotter end of the spectrum, the more helpful it will be to jot down the answers to some of these questions as you develop your story.

Story Questions

What is the working title for this story?

This story is about:

The kind of emotional experience I want to give my readers is:

If your model book creates an emotional experience similar to the one you're trying to create in your own novel, you might spend a little time contemplating how the author manipulated your emotions as their story unfolded.

The point of this story—the thing I want the reader to get from reading it—is:

What are my favorite books?

What things do these books have in common?
Consider characters, settings, types of stories, emotions you experienced while reading them, and types of events. How might you incorporate some of these elements into your own story?

Character Questions

Protagonist: main character or hero/ine of the story. In romance, the heroine is often the protagonist.
My protagonist is:

My protagonist wants:

My protagonist needs:

My protagonist has been shaped by the following past events:

My protagonist's weakness or flaw is:

Other important details about my protagonist:

Physical appearance, quirks, personality traits, beliefs, cultural background, possessions, and special skills/abilities.

Antagonist: the villain of the story, or the person who is actively opposing the protagonist. In romance, sometimes the antagonist is the hero.

My antagonist is:

My antagonist wants:

My antagonist needs:

My antagonist has been shaped by the following past events:

My antagonist's weakness or flaw is:

Other important details about my antagonist:

Physical appearance, quirks, personality traits, beliefs, cultural background, possessions, and special skills/abilities.

Contagonist: a main character who creates problems for the protagonist but isn't necessarily a villain/antagonist. Could be a mentor, an ally, or a love interest. The contagonist may both help and hinder the protagonist. In romance, the contagonist is often the hero. *(Not all stories have a contagonist.)*

My contagonist is:

My contagonist wants:

My contagonist needs:

My contagonist has been shaped by the following past events:

My contagonist's weakness or flaw is:

Other important details about my contagonist:

Physical appearance, quirks, personality traits, beliefs, cultural background, possessions, and special skills/abilities.

Other characters in my story:

Some of these will be obvious—if your protagonist visits a library, you may need a librarian—and others will only occur to you as you're writing.

Other characters, continued...

Relationship Questions

This section assumes that the protagonist and contagonist are the couple falling in love; adjust the questions accordingly if this isn't true in your story.

What is the protagonist's first impression of the contagonist?

What does the protagonist like about the contagonist?

What does the protagonist not like about the contagonist?

How does the protagonist's opinion of the contagonist change by the climax of the story?

How is the protagonist forced to work with the contagonist?

In what ways would the protagonist prefer to work against the contagonist?

What is the contagonist's first impression of the protagonist?

What does the contagonist like about the protagonist?

What does the contagonist not like about the protagonist?

How does the contagonist's opinion of the protagonist change by the climax of the story?

How is the contagonist forced to work with the protagonist?

In what ways would the contagonist prefer to work against the protagonist?

What do the protagonist and contagonist disagree about?

What do the protagonist and contagonist agree on?

As the protagonist changes, how does s/he become more compatible with the contagonist?

As the contagonist changes, how does s/he become more compatible with the protagonist?

By the climax of the story, what would the protagonist sacrifice for the contagonist?

By the climax of the story, what would the contagonist sacrifice for the protagonist?

How will you show or hint that the protagonist and contagonist will live happily-ever-after (happily-for-now) at the end of this story?

Setting Questions

My story takes place in/at:

The things I find intriguing about this location are:

How do each of my main characters fit into this setting or have trouble fitting into it?
Protagonist:

Antagonist:

Contagonist:

Is there anything unusual about this setting?

How do I feel about this setting?

What potential problems could this setting cause for each of my main characters?

Protagonist:

Antagonist:

Contagonist:

What is each main character's attitude toward this setting?

Protagonist:

Antagonist:

Contagonist:

Plot Questions

What events do I want to happen in this story?

What types of events do I love to read about—either in fiction or in the news?

Might any of these events fit into the story I'm telling?

How might my protagonist be in conflict with:

Other people:

Society's laws or unwritten rules:

His/her environment:

Himself or herself:

Do any of these conflicts give rise to things that might happen in my story?

How might my antagonist be in conflict with:

Other people:

Society's laws or unwritten rules:

His/her environment:

Himself or herself:

Do any of these conflicts give rise to things that might happen in my story?

How might my contagonist be in conflict with:

Other people:

Society's laws or unwritten rules:

His/her environment:

Himself or herself:

Do any of these conflicts give rise to things that might happen in my story?

The Beginning

Also known as Act I.

What are some interesting ways that my story might start?

What are some intriguing ways that I might introduce the reader to my protagonist?

What are some interesting ways I might introduce my reader to my antagonist?

What are some intriguing ways that I might introduce the reader to my contagonist?

What are the worst things that could possibly happen to my protagonist?

What are the worst things that could possibly happen to my contagonist?

What are the best things that could possibly happen to my antagonist?

What are the first things my protagonist and contagonist might try to solve their problems?

What additional problems might the protagonist and contagonist create as they try to solve their problems?

What kinds of things might my antagonist be doing at the start of the story that could cause problems for my protagonist and contagonist?

How might the protagonist and contagonist react to what the antagonist does in the early part of the story?

What bigger mess do the protagonist and contagonist find themselves in as a result of tangling with the antagonist at the beginning of this story?

The Middle

Also known as Act II.

- What sort of journey do the protagonist and contagonist go on as a result of the big mess they find themselves in at the end of this story's beginning?
- Where are they trying to go?
- What obstacles stand between them and their destination?

Act II obstacle brainstorming continued...

How could the protagonist (and contagonist) try to overcome each of these obstacles? For each possible obstacle, will they succeed or fail?

What do the protagonist and contagonist need to realize in order to reach their destination?

What situation causes the protagonist and contagonist to realize this?

How does realizing this change the protagonist's and contagonist's behavior?

The End

Also known as Act III.

Do the protagonist and contagonist succeed or fail in reaching their destination or achieving their goal?

How might the protagonist and contagonist defeat the antagonist? Or if the antagonist wins, how might s/he defeat the protagonist and contagonist?
This is the climax of your story.

How might each character react to the climax?

Protagonist:

Antagonist:

Contagonist:

Other characters in the story:

What happens to all the characters at the end of this story?

Creating a Plot Outline

You've brainstormed a lot of possible events for your story. If you're closer to the plotter end of the spectrum, you may want to start inserting some of those events into your plot outline before you start writing (in pencil, so it can be updated).

If you're using the *Before You Write* prompts to write your novel, you don't necessarily need to fill this outline in beforehand. The prompts are designed to guide you through a solid story structure while drawing on the ideas you came up with during brainstorming.

I recommend that you use this outline to briefly record what you wrote each day.

If you're <u>not</u> using the *Before Your Write* prompts but are working off your own plot outline instead, you might try to break it down into thirty chunks, so you'll have a rough idea what you're going to be writing about each day.

For those not using the prompts, I still recommend that you record what you write each day in the plot outline or update your outline. Once filled out, this simple plot outline will give you the big picture of your story, which you'll need for editing. It'll also be the basis for the synopsis you'll send out to editors and agents after the novel is polished and ready to submit.

Act One

1.

2.

3.

4.

5.

6.

7.

Act Two

8.

9.

10.

11.

12.

13.

14.

15.

16.

17.

18.

19.

20.

21.

22.

23.

Act Three

24.

25.

26.

27.

28.

29.

30.

Filling in the Holes

It's not unusual to have some difficulty figuring out what happens in your story.

What can you do when that happens?

Look to Your Characters

Review your characters' goals, motivations, flaws, backstory and personality traits. Sometimes reminding yourself what the characters want and need will bring insight into what they might do next.

Puzzle It Out

It's common to figure out some of the big story events first, and then go back and figure out how to connect them. The brainstorming we've already talked about is a great way to generate those big events.

How do you figure out what happens in the gaps between those big events?

Let's say that your protagonist is an archaeologist, and you know that he's going to discover a lost tomb containing a magical artifact that he'll have to risk his life to retrieve.

And you know that later, your antagonist is going to ambush him and steal the artifact.

How do you get your protagonist from the tomb to the site of the ambush?

First, ask yourself: "What is the aftermath of the first event?"

In the process of retrieving the artifact, did your protagonist injure himself? Lose something important? Learn something new about the artifact or the danger he's in?

How does he feel about having violated the ancient tomb? What does he intend to do with the artifact? Does he believe in the ancient curse that was inscribed on the wall of the tomb?

Does he have to go somewhere to get medical treatment or can he patch himself up?

Did he attract the attention of the antagonist, and if so, is the antagonist doing anything in response that might affect the protagonist?

Is there really a curse, and if so, what's happening as a result of it being focused on the protagonist? How is his concern about being cursed affecting his behavior? If he doesn't believe in the curse, do those around him, and if so, does it affect how they treat him?

Now that the protagonist has the artifact, what does he plan to do with it? Get it to a museum? Have a wizard neutralize it? Sell it to someone who will use its powers for good?

Second, ask yourself: "What has to happen to set up the second event?"

Your protagonist has to have a reason to be in the place where the antagonist will ambush him. Why's he there? Is he trying to show the artifact to an appraiser or a wizard or another archaeologist? Is he trying to get the curse lifted?

Also, how did the antagonist know he'd be there? Is the contagonist or some secondary character spying on the protagonist for the antagonist? Does the antagonist have the ability to track the artifact with magic?

How did the protagonist get to the ambush site, and what could go wrong on the way? Could the curse be causing problems that slow him down? Could his superstitious belief in a curse cause him to take a less-than-optimal route? Could he be betrayed by someone along the way? What dangers lie along his chosen route?

Does the protagonist know that the antagonist wants the artifact? If so, is he preparing to defend it? Or trying to find out what the antagonist is up to as he travels to the ambush site? Does he have allies he can visit to request help?

If you think about the fallout from the first event and how your character might react to it, as well as the things that have to be set up for your next big scene, you'll start to get ideas for filling in the holes in your plot outline.

Dream Your Plot

You can also try this dream technique for sparking inspiration. Science fiction author Ray Bradbury used to identify a question at the end of his daily writing session that he needed answered. Before he fell asleep each night, he would repeat that question over and over. Often, the next morning he would wake up knowing the answer to his question.

For example, let's say that your protagonist has been kidnapped by your antagonist, and you haven't been able to figure out how he'll escape.

Before bed, ask yourself: *How could Clark escape from Frank's basement without Frank knowing?*

It can take a little bit of practice before you and your subconscious get used to working together like this, so if you don't get an answer the first night, give yourself several more nights of repetition.

Also, there's no rule that says you have to write every scene of your novel in order. If you need some time to figure out a story problem, it's okay to put in a placeholder scene, and write it later once you've solved the problem:

[Clark escapes from Frank's basement, and steals the Etruscan artifact.]*

Don't forget to put an asterisk next to your placeholder so that it's easy to search for when you're ready to come back to it.

Problems as Inspiration

A story where things happen randomly to the characters tends to be episodic and unsatisfying—it's crucial that readers understand *why* each event in the story is happening. If the events of the middle aren't connected to the events in the beginning of the story in some way, your story will lose cohesion.

Mystery author Raymond Chandler used to say:

"When in doubt, have a man come through a door with a gun in his hand."

In other words, if you don't know what happens next in your story, give your character a new problem to solve.

BUT...

...make sure that this new problem arises in some way from what's already happened. The man with the gun in his hand might be someone that the protagonist frustrated in a previous scene. Or someone that the antagonist hired after learning about the protagonist's earlier actions. Or a third party who found out about the protagonist's intentions and decided to intervene.

Continuing our example from before, maybe the man with the gun is an antique dealer who learned about the artifact when the protagonist came to him for information about the tomb. Or maybe the man with the gun is one of the tomb's guardians, brought back to life by the curse that the protagonist activated by stealing the artifact.

If you think of a cool problem to throw at the protagonist that doesn't arise from what's already happened in the story, make a note to yourself to add the necessary setup scene when you revise your novel.

How to Use This Journal

The rest of this book walks you through the process of writing your novel one day at a time.

Each day's entry contains a *Before You Write* and an *After You Write* section.

Before You Write

If you're an experienced writer and you've already got a plotting method that works for you, great! If you're a newer writer and not entirely sure yet how to plot a story, the daily prompts will help you come up with a story that follows basic three act structure.

Each journal entry starts with a rough idea of where you should be in your story, along with a few optional brainstorming questions. I strongly recommend that you write out your answers to each day's *Before You Write* questions either the night before, right before you go to sleep, or some time before your planned writing session for that day. Even if you don't have time to sit down and write out the answers to the next day's questions before bed, you can still benefit by reading the questions out loud before you go to sleep—this is a great technique for getting your subconscious started on the next day's scenes, and it only takes a minute or two.

Each day's questions should take between fifteen and thirty minutes to answer, although you can certainly spend more time if you like. It may help you focus to set a timer—five minutes per question—and freewrite your answer.

You may find that some of the brainstorming questions for a particular day, while relevant to your story, don't apply to the scene(s) you're writing that day. That's okay—it just means you're figuring out some aspects of the story a little bit in advance.

Also, you may find that your answers sometimes diverge from the question as you freewrite. That's great! The point of these questions is to spark your creativity and help you understand your characters more deeply. It's inevitable that the answers to some questions will take you to unexpected places in your characters' psyches.

Some writers prefer to write their stories in order, but if you're one of those writers who sometimes skips around as inspiration strikes, it's fine to switch to a different day's prompts, and come back to the current day later. The good think about the prompts, though, is that if you take the time to answers the *Before You Write* questions, chances are you *won't* get stuck.

Depending on the needs of your story, you may wish to rearrange the order of the days in Act One (i.e. maybe you need to introduce your contagonist or your antagonist before your protagonist shows up). However, the brainstorming prompts in Act Two and Act Three are very carefully constructed to make sure your story's middle doesn't sag and that the romantic relationship develops in a believable way that's tied in with the characters' growth arcs, so that by the time you reach the story's climax, you've got the reader on the edge of their seat. Think very carefully about the dramatic impact of switching the order of the prompts in these parts of the story before you change them.

If you find that you cannot answer all questions on a particular day, you may wish to move them forward to the next day or go back to them later in the story, when they feel relevant to what you are writing.

And finally, it's possible that the days won't correspond precisely with your writing days because of the way you'll prefer to emphasize events. Maybe the parts of your story that fall on days 15 and 16 will be relatively brief, but your day 19 will be a massive chapter that takes three writing sessions to get through. This story blueprint is a flexible guide to move you through effective story structure, not a hard-and-fast formula that your story must conform to. Whenever you need to take more time to do a scene justice, do so, even if it means you need thirty-five days to finish your novel.

Where do these questions come from?

This story blueprint is adapted from the hero's journey, but tweaked to fit the journey of two people falling in love, and is designed to help you fully flesh out the progression of your characters' relationship.

This story blueprint assumes that you'll have a single protagonist, a contagonist, and an antagonist. In a heterosexual romance, the heroine is often the protagonist, and the hero is usually either the contagonist or the antagonist (depending on what kind of story you want to tell).

If your story doesn't include a contagonist, or if the antagonist is not a person but a force of nature or a situation (like having a disease) or an internal obstacle, you'll need to adjust each day's action accordingly.

I assume that your protagonist and contagonist stick together throughout the story once they've met.

A contagonist's role in the story is to keep the protagonist honest and paying attention, as well as to provoke the protagonist to face fears and overcome his/her flaw...if these two aren't together for the majority of the story, it's tough for the contagonist to do his/her job.

If your protagonist and contagonist won't be working together throughout the story, you'll have to tweak for when they separate, what each is doing when they're not together, and when they reunite.

I also assume that your novel doesn't have a subplot. If you're planning to include a subplot, you'll need to use your judgment in adding additional scenes throughout the story, or including the events of the subplot in the main story. If this is your first novel, I recommend skipping the subplot and focusing on telling a simple story well.

When I refer to the antagonist's minions or forces, I don't just mean people who are working for the antagonist full-time.

Minions can refer to anyone who's helping the antagonist in the moment, even if it's a government official who the antagonist has bribed to look the other way or a neutral party whose behavior helps the antagonist, like a police officer who stops the protagonist from breaking into the antagonist's apartment to foil his/her evil plan.

If a secondary character is acting in a way that favors the antagonist, intentionally or not, you can use them in a "minion" position.

Also, inanimate objects, forces of nature, and other sources of conflict which aren't under the control of the antagonist but whose effects favor the antagonist can go in the "minion" or "antagonist's forces" position.

When I use the words "fight" or "battle", this encompasses any type of conflict that might arise between the protagonist's forces (including contagonist) and the antagonist and his/her forces.

This could refer to a literal battle, but the conflict doesn't have to be physical. If part of the protagonist's plan to defeat the antagonist involves embarrassing the antagonist by revealing one of the antagonist's secrets to the antagonist's mother, for example, this scene, along with the antagonist's response to the revelation, can be considered one of the battles they fight.

This isn't the only way to apply the hero's journey, and there are a lot of great books out there which offer other models. If the way I apply the hero's journey and the character growth arc to three-act structure doesn't work for you, I encourage you to explore other approaches.

Also, the hero's journey isn't the only way to plot. Here are some fantastic books on plotting—if you're like me, you'll end up reading several and synthesizing them into a model of story structure that works for you.

- **Beginnings, Middles and Ends**, by Nancy Kress
  One of the best books I've ever read about three-act structure and how stories work.

- **Create a Plot Clinic,** by Holly Lisle
  Fantastic exercises for discovering the conflicts that will serve as the foundation of your plot. I also strongly recommend her *Create a Character Clinic* and *Create a Culture Clinic*.
- **Break Into Fiction,** by Mary Buckham and Dianna Love
  Based on the hero's journey but compatible with three-act structure, this book contains a series of worksheets that show you how to weave character and plot together. Highly recommended for romance writers.
- **Story Physics,** by Larry Brooks
  Explains, in great detail, all the major plot points in a functional story and how they work together to create a plot that your readers will love.
- **Plot**, by Ansen Dibell
  A must-read classic on how to put scenes together to make a story.
- **Fiction Writer's Brainstormer,** by James V. Smith Jr.
  Fantastic book—Smith will take you through brainstorming your plot (and characters) at the macro and micro level.

Here are some resources specific to the romance genre:

- **TV Tropes' List of Romance Tropes**
  Not to be missed--a witty examination of a romance tropes that will stimulate your thinking about your story (also a great brainstorming resource when you're stuck!): http://tvtropes.org/pmwiki/pmwiki.php/Main/Romance Arc

- **Virginia Kantra's Developing the Romance in Your Romance Novel**

  This one is a fairly-comprehensive overview of things you'll need to consider when writing your romance-- highly-recommended:

  http://virginiakantra.net/romancearticle.html

- **The 12 Stages of Intimacy**

  As you're working through each day of your story, you'll want to show the progression of the romance through physical intimacy (or lack thereof). Here's a helpful article on the 12 stages and how to use them to increase tension:

  http://jennyhansenauthor.wordpress.com/2011/11/08/usi ng-the-12-stages-of-physical-intimacy-to-build-tension- in-your-novel/

- **Six Steps to Stronger Character Arcs**

  Don't miss Joan McCollum's article on how to build stronger character arcs in a romance: http://romanceuniversity.org/2013/08/02/jordan- mccollum-six-steps-to-stronger-character-arcs-in- romances/

- **Dummies Guide to Romance Heroines**

  Lots of great tips here for heroine-building:

  http://www.dummies.com/how-to/content/discovering- the-key-to-every-romance-novel-the-her.html

- **Adrienne de Wolfe's 20 Tips for Writing Loveable Romance Novel Heroes**
  Excellent article on how to construct a hero that your readers can fall in love with easily:
  http://www.thecreativepenn.com/2012/07/01/writing-romance-heroes/
- **The Lovers Journey,** by Deborah M. Hale:
  http://www.deborahhale.com/mobiletipjourney.htm
- **The Hero's Journey for Romance Writers**, by Colleen Gleason:
  http://theindievoice.com/for-writers/writing-technique/the-heros-journey-for-romance-writers/

An article that you may find helpful if your romance will have a mystery plot:

- **The Hero's Journey, Mystery Style**, by Melissa Bourbon Ramirez:
  http://misaramirez.com/for-writers/the-heros-journey-mystery-style/

After You Write

The **Before You Write** section for each day serves as a guide to approximately where you should be in your story that day.

The **After You Write** section helps you identify and eliminate obstacles to writing, so that you can develop the kind of writing habit that the pros have.

Even experienced writers may benefit from answering the **After You Write** questions, as they will help you further refine your creative process.

You'll be asked to record your progress and to answer a

couple of questions about what worked and what didn't.

As you work through this 30-day program, you'll start to notice what conditions help you write more easily and what conditions might be slowing you down.

One of the things you'll be asked to do is note any negative thoughts that you had about writing, and to reframe them as positive thoughts.

Many psychological studies show (my personal experience backs this up) that noticing your negative thoughts and taking a few moments to restate them positively will, over time, reduce the frequency of negative thoughts you experience and increase the number of positive thoughts.

Since those negative thoughts are a primary cause of procrastination, doing your daily reframes is a way of inoculating yourself against the desire to procrastinate.

Here's an example of how reframing works:

Negative thought: I'm a terrible writer.
Positive thought: I'm learning how to become a better writer.

Negative thought: This novel sucks. No one will ever want to read it.
Positive thought: This is a rough draft, so it's too early to tell if it sucks. Once it's finished, I'll get some help with editing it.

Negative thought: This is too hard, I'll never manage to write an entire novel.
Positive thought: If I stick with this program, I will finish my

novel on Day 30.

It's easy to generate reasons to give up, and your inner critic is going to throw lots of them at you. If you can learn to reframe your excuses and discouraging thoughts positively, you'll find that it gets easier and easier to stick with the writing.

Progress Tracker

My story will be _____ words long.

	Today's Word Count	Total Word Count
Day 1		
Day 2		
Day 3		
Day 4		
Day 5		
Day 6		
Day 7		
Day 8		
Day 9		
Day 10		
Day 11		
Day 12		
Day 13		
Day 14		
Day 15		

My daily word count goal is _____ words/day.

	Today's Word Count	Total Word Count
Day 16		
Day 17		
Day 18		
Day 19		
Day 20		
Day 21		
Day 22		
Day 23		
Day 24		
Day 25		
Day 26		
Day 27		
Day 28		
Day 29		
Day 30		

Day 1

The secret of getting ahead is getting started.
—Mark Twain

Before You Write

This is the day you introduce your readers to your protagonist. You'll want to give them a taste of your protagonist's everyday life (their ordinary world), and show or hint at your protagonist's flaw (the flaw they will overcome by the end of the story). You'll also want to show or hint how the protagonist's flaw is causing him/her to be single or to stay in a relationship that's wrong for him/her, and how this is less-than-ideal.

You'll also want to either introduce a change into the protagonist's life, or hint at the change that's coming. This change should present itself as a problem: it could be a problem that the protagonist is excited to solve, or one that s/he's upset about. This problem will pit him/her against the antagonist and/or the contagonist (love interest).

Depending on your story's premise, you may or may not want to show the protagonist meeting the antagonist or contagonist—it's your call. If the protagonist and love interest meet, it's crucial that they have strong reactions to each other, whether positive or negative.

Brainstorming questions

What do you think the reader will find most interesting about your protagonist?

What is unique about your protagonist?

What is your protagonist's flaw or wound?

What traumatic event(s) created that flaw or wound?

How is it keeping him/her single or in a relationship that's wrong for him/her?

How does the protagonist feel about his/her current relationship status, and what does s/he do to cope with this less-than-ideal situation?

What does the protagonist want from a romantic partner? What does s/he need from a romantic partner?

What change (i.e. problem) will you hint at or introduce in your protagonist's life?

What is his/her first reaction to this change?

How will the contagonist and the antagonist help or hinder the protagonist's attempts to solve this problem?

What is it about the contagonist that rubs the protagonist the wrong way?

What is it about the contagonist that the protagonist finds attractive?

What other characters does the protagonist interact with?

After You Write

How many words did you write today?

How did it go?

Did you write at your scheduled time? If not, why not? When did you write instead? Why was this a better time?

Did you experience any distractions while you were writing?

How could you prevent those distractions from arising again? Or if they aren't avoidable, how could you minimize their impact on your writing in the future?

Did you experience any negative thoughts about writing at any time today?

Can you reframe those thoughts positively?

Day 2

Writing a novel is like driving at night. You can only see as far as your headlights let you, but you can make the whole trip that way.
    —E.L. Doctorow

Before You Write

Today you will introduce the contagonist (love interest) and give the reader a taste of contagonist's everyday life. You'll show or hint at the contagonist's flaw or wound, and give the reader a glimpse into why that flaw or wound is causing the contagonist to remain single or in a relationship that is wrong for him/her, and why this is less than ideal.

You'll also want to either introduce a change into the contagonist's life, or hint at the change that's coming. This change should present itself as a problem: it could be a problem that the protagonist is excited to solve, or one that s/he's upset about. This problem may be triggered by meeting the protagonist, and it will the contagonist against the antagonist and/or the protagonist. If this change can trigger the protagonist's flaw, even better.

If contagonist did not meet the protagonist yesterday, they

might meet today.

Brainstorming questions

What do you think the reader will find most interesting about your contagonist?

What is unique about your contagonist?

What is your contagonist's flaw or wound?

What traumatic event(s) created that flaw or wound?

How is it keeping him/her single or in a relationship that's wrong for him/her?

How does the contagonist feel about his/her current relationship status, and what does s/he do to cope with this less-than-ideal situation?

What does the contagonist want from a romantic partner? What does s/he need from a romantic partner?

What change (i.e. problem) will you hint at or introduce in your contagonist's life?

What is his/her first reaction to this change?

What is the contagonist's plan for dealing with this change?

How is the contagonist's flaw making it harder for him/her to deal with this change?

How will the protagonist and/or antagonist oppose the contagonist's attempts to solve this problem?

What is it about the protagonist that rubs the contagonist the wrong way?

What is it about the protagonist that the contagonist finds attractive?

While this is happening, what is the antagonist doing?

After You Write

How many words did you write today?

How did it go?

Did you write at your scheduled time? If not, why not? When did you write instead? Why was this a better time?

Did you experience any distractions while you were writing?

How could you prevent those distractions from arising again? Or if they aren't avoidable, how could you minimize their impact on your writing in the future?

Did you experience any negative thoughts about writing at any time today?

Can you reframe those thoughts positively?

Day 3

There are probably as many ways to get started as there are ways of chasing the blues. Use anything that works, even if it seems ridiculous or not what an artist does.
  —Anna Held Audette

Before You Write

If they haven't already, your protagonist and contagonist should meet as a result of trying to resolve their respective problems. If they have already met, this second meeting will include each one's reaction to the previous meeting.

You'll need to show or hint at how their respective story problems cause them to be in conflict, and how those problems have gotten worse or more complicated as a result of these two characters interacting.

If it hasn't shown up in the story yet, make sure the reader sees their primary relationship conflict here (i.e. how their respective flaws cause them to not get along in some way). Let the reader see their attraction to each other, and their reactions to that attraction.

If the protagonist and contagonist encounter the antagonist, show or hint at the antagonist's goal and/or his/her motivation for pursuing that goal.

Brainstorming questions

How do the protagonist and contagonist meet? How are they in conflict with each other during this meeting?

Are they both attracted to each other, or is the attraction one-sided?

How is that attraction affecting their interaction with each other?

Do the protagonist and contagonist have a reason to work together yet?

Do the protagonist and contagonist have reasons they would rather not work together?

How do their problems get worse or more complicated as a result of their interaction?

How do their goals change or shift as a result of their interaction?

If the antagonist is present, what is s/he doing?

After You Write

How many words did you write today?

How did it go?

Did you write at your scheduled time? If not, why not? When did you write instead? Why was this a better time?

Did you experience any distractions while you were writing?

How could you prevent those distractions from arising again? Or if they aren't avoidable, how could you minimize their impact on your writing in the future?

Did you experience any negative thoughts about writing at any time today?

Can you reframe those thoughts positively?

Day 4

Opportunity is missed by most people because it is dressed in overalls and looks like work.
      —*Thomas Edison*

Before You Write

Today's the day you introduce your antagonist, if you haven't already. If your antagonist has appeared in earlier scenes, this is where you give the reader a taste of the antagonist's everyday life and how s/he sees him/herself.

If you are introducing the antagonist through his/her minions or through the aftereffects of his/her actions (for example, your protagonist and contagonist are standing in the smoking crater the antagonist has left behind), you might reveal these things through speculation and discussion of what the other characters know about the antagonist.

Show or hint at how the antagonist will be making life harder for the protagonist and/or contagonist. This is also a great place to show or hint at the antagonist's motives for pursuing his/her goal, and to show or hint at the antagonist's flaw, which will lead to his/her defeat at the hands of the protagonist and contagonist.

If the protagonist and/or contagonist are present, show or hint at how the antagonist sees them.

(If it's too early in the story to reveal the antagonist, that's okay--move on to Day 5 for now, and come back to the Day 4 instructions when it is time for the antagonist to appear. Don't delay too long, though: if you introduce the antagonist too late in the story, the reader will feel cheated.)

Brainstorming questions

What is special or unique about your antagonist? How will you communicate that to the reader?

What is your antagonist's flaw or wound? What traumatic event(s) created that flaw or wound? How does it keep him/her making the wrong choices in life?

What problem will your antagonist be trying to solve over the course of this story?

How will the protagonist be opposing the antagonist's attempts to solve this problem?

How will the contagonist be opposing the antagonist's attempts to solve this problem?

What is it about the protagonist that rubs the antagonist the wrong way?

What is it about the contagonist that rubs the antagonist the wrong way?

If the protagonist and/or contagonist are present, what are they doing?

After You Write

How many words did you write today?

How did it go?

Did you write at your scheduled time? If not, why not? When did you write instead? Why was this a better time?

Did you experience any distractions while you were writing?

How could you prevent those distractions from arising again? Or if they aren't avoidable, how could you minimize their impact on your writing in the future?

Did you experience any negative thoughts about writing at any time today?

Can you reframe those thoughts positively?

Day 5

The ideal way to work on a project is to ask a question you don't know the answer to.
—*Francis Ford Coppola*

Before You Write

The protagonist reacts to his/her interactions with the contagonist so far. Reasons why a relationship with the contagonist are a bad idea are considered. S/he comes to a conclusion about how s/he will treat the contagonist (i.e. ignore, fight, or pursue the attraction).

The protagonist also reacts to his/her interactions with the antagonist, if any, and identifies new obstacles related to his/her story problem.

The protagonist's flaw becomes more visible here, and affects his/her feelings about the other characters, as well as his/her chances of solving his/her story problem.

The protagonist may seek advice from a trusted source or look for guidance within. S/he comes up with a new plan for solving his/her story problem, and takes the first small step in executing that plan.

If the contagonist and/or antagonist are present, they may

help or hinder the protagonist.

Whether the antagonist is present or not, s/he takes a step to solve his/her own story problem, which may affect the protagonist/contagonist now or in the future. (You should always know what your absent antagonist is up to.)

Brainstorming questions

What is the protagonist's reaction to his/her interactions with the contagonist and the antagonist?

How is the protagonist's flaw/wound affecting his/her thinking?

How does the contagonist react to the protagonist's flaw?

What guidance, if any, does the protagonist receive before creating his/her new plan?

What is the protagonist's new plan?

What is the first step the protagonist takes to solve his/her problems?

If the contagonist is present, how does s/he help or hinder?

If the antagonist is present, how does s/he help or hinder?

After You Write

How many words did you write today?

How did it go?

Did you write at your scheduled time? If not, why not? When did you write instead? Why was this a better time?

Did you experience any distractions while you were writing?

How could you prevent those distractions from arising again? Or if they aren't avoidable, how could you minimize their impact on your writing in the future?

Did you experience any negative thoughts about writing at any time today?

Can you reframe those thoughts positively?

Day 6

If everything seems under control, you're just not going fast enough.
—Mario Andretti

Before You Write

The contagonist reacts to his/her interactions with the protagonist so far. Reasons why a relationship with the contagonist are a bad idea are considered. S/he comes to a conclusion about how s/he will treat the protagonist (i.e. ignore, fight, or pursue the attraction).

The contagonist also reacts to his/her interactions with the antagonist, if any, and identifies new obstacles related to his/her story problem.

The contagonist's flaw becomes more visible and affects his/her feelings about the other characters and about his/her chances of solving his/her story problem.

The contagonist may seek advice from a trusted source or look within for guidance. S/he comes up with a new plan for solving his/her story problem, and takes the first small step in executing that plan.

The protagonist and/or antagonist may or may not be present. If either is present, they may help or hinder the contagonist. If the antagonist is not present, s/he is still up to no good.

Brainstorming questions

What is the contagonist's reaction to his/her interactions with the protagonist and antagonist?

How is the contagonist's flaw/wound affecting his/her thinking?

How does the protagonist react to the contagonist's flaw?

What guidance, if any, does the contagonist receive?

What is the contagonist's new plan?

What is the first step in the contagonist's new plan?

If the protagonist is present, how does s/he help or hinder?

If the antagonist is present, how does s/he help or hinder?

After You Write

How many words did you write today?

How did it go?

Did you write at your scheduled time? If not, why not? When did you write instead? Why was this a better time?

Did you experience any distractions while you were writing?

How could you prevent those distractions from arising again? Or if they aren't avoidable, how could you minimize their impact on your writing in the future?

Did you experience any negative thoughts about writing at any time today?

Can you reframe those thoughts positively?

Day 7

The desire to write grows with writing.
    —Erasmus

Before You Write

The protagonist's and contagonist's attempts to execute their respective plans bring them together. Whether one or both succeeds or fails in what they are trying to do, the result is to force them together in some way (i.e. they must become allies, they are stuck together in close quarters, they are the only two candidates in competition for a single prize, etc).

Each of them may accept or refuse to accept that they are effectively yoked together until their story problem can be resolved.

Whatever their respective reactions to being forced together, these reactions put them in conflict with each other (i.e. personal attacks, disagreement about how to proceed, negotiation for how they will or will not work together, etc). Their respective flaws will make this conflict worse.

The protagonist and contagonist realize that in order to solve their respective problems, they will have to enter new territory. (It's fine if this is only new territory for one of the characters, for example, the hero is an FBI agent but the heroine has never had to go into hiding before.

However, at some point soon, the situation will need to change drastically enough that the other character also finds themself in new territory, for example, perhaps going into hiding means foregoing the usual FBI resources in order to keep a mole from ratting them out.) It's also fine if the new territory isn't physical (i.e. the new territory is that protagonist and contagonist, who used to run competing departments, are now being forced to work together on a new task force).

If the antagonist is present, s/he may help or hinder either of the other two characters, and may do things to drive a wedge between them.

Whether the antagonist is present or not, s/he takes a step to solve his/her own story problem, which may affect the protagonist/contagonist now or in the future.

Brainstorming questions

How do the protagonist and contagonist come together? Are they working with each other or working against each other?

Does each one succeed or fail in achieving their short-term goal (i.e. the thing they're trying to do right now)?

In what way are the protagonist and contagonist yoked together as a result of these events?

What are their reactions to being yoked together?

What is the new territory they will need to explore in order to solve their respective problems?

If the antagonist is present, how does s/he help or hinder?

What is the antagonist doing to solve his/her own problems right now?

After You Write

How many words did you write today?

How did it go?

Did you write at your scheduled time? If not, why not? When did you write instead? Why was this a better time?

Did you experience any distractions while you were writing?

How could you prevent those distractions from arising again? Or if they aren't avoidable, how could you minimize their impact on your writing in the future?

Did you experience any negative thoughts about writing at any time today?

Can you reframe those thoughts positively?

Day 8

Courage is resistance to fear, mastery of fear, not absence of fear.
—Mark Twain

Before You Write

The protagonist and contagonist explore new territory. At least one of them is off-balance and has difficulty adjusting. Their exploration of the new territory makes it even more obvious that they cannot afford to split up.

Protagonist and contagonist still disagree, but have come to a temporary truce for the sake of defeating the antagonist.

If the antagonist is present, s/he may help or hinder either of the other two characters, and may do things to drive a wedge between them.

Whether the antagonist is present or not, s/he takes a step to solve his/her own story problem, which may affect the protagonist/contagonist now or in the future.

Brainstorming questions

How are the protagonist and contagonist adapting to the new territory?

In what ways are the protagonist and contagonist off-balance?

In what ways do the protagonist and contagonist agree?

In what ways do they disagree?

What new problems does the new territory throw at the protagonist and contagonist?

Is the antagonist present? What is s/he doing right now?

After You Write

How many words did you write today?

How did it go?

Did you write at your scheduled time? If not, why not? When did you write instead? Why was this a better time?

Did you experience any distractions while you were writing?

How could you prevent those distractions from arising again? Or if they aren't avoidable, how could you minimize their impact on your writing in the future?

Did you experience any negative thoughts about writing at any time today?

Can you reframe those thoughts positively?

Day 9

The seed of the idea is developed by both labor and the unconscious, and the struggle that goes on between them.
  —Carson McCullers

Before You Write

The protagonist and/or contagonist start to get the hang of the new territory. They make progress toward their goals. They may help or hinder each other.

As the protagonist and contagonist observe each other, they each notice and react to at least one thing that changes their opinion of the other positively and increases their attraction to the other. They may or may not become aware of each others' flaw.

If the antagonist is present, s/he may help or hinder either of the other two characters, and may do things to drive a wedge between them.

Whether the antagonist is present or not, s/he takes a step to solve his/her own story problem, which may affect the protagonist/contagonist now or in the future.

Brainstorming questions

In what ways are the protagonist and contagonist getting better at navigating the new territory? What are they still struggling with?

As the protagonist and contagonist watch each other struggle, how do their opinions of each other change for the positive? For the negative?

Is the antagonist present? What is s/he doing right now?

After You Write

How many words did you write today?

How did it go?

Did you write at your scheduled time? If not, why not? When did you write instead? Why was this a better time?

Did you experience any distractions while you were writing?

How could you prevent those distractions from arising again? Or if they aren't avoidable, how could you minimize their impact on your writing in the future?

Did you experience any negative thoughts about writing at any time today?

Can you reframe those thoughts positively?

Day 10

The best way out is always through.
 —Robert Frost

Before You Write

Being in an unfamiliar world, the protagonist and/or contagonist forget to take something into account, and stumbles into trouble. The characters' flaws contributes to the stumble.

Because things aren't going well and the characters' partnership is new, any stumbles or glitches should trigger the conflict in their relationship (i.e. the ways in which they are not compatible). They may argue or they may try to hide/ignore their negative reactions for the sake of making progress.

If the antagonist is present, s/he may help or hinder either of the other two characters, and may do things to drive a wedge between them. Whether the antagonist is present or not, s/he takes a step to solve his/her own story problem, which may affect the protagonist/contagonist now or in the future. (You may or may not show it, but you should always know what your absent antagonist is up to.)

Brainstorming questions

What aspect of the new territory causes the protagonist and/or contagonist to make a mistake?

How does the character's flaw/wound contribute to the mistake or make it worse?

How does the protagonist react to this mistake?

How does the contagonist react to this mistake?

How does this mistake trigger the conflict inherent in their relationship (i.e. make their incompatibilities obvious)?

Is the antagonist present? What is s/he doing right now?

After You Write

How many words did you write today?

How did it go?

Did you write at your scheduled time? If not, why not? When did you write instead? Why was this a better time?

Did you experience any distractions while you were writing?

How could you prevent those distractions from arising again? Or if they aren't avoidable, how could you minimize their impact on your writing in the future?

Did you experience any negative thoughts about writing at any time today?

Can you reframe those thoughts positively?

Day 11

...one of the ways you keep on writing is by pausing every once in a while and daydreaming about how nice it will be when the book is finished and published.
—Cory Doctorow

Before You Write

The protagonist and contagonist disagree in some way on how to get out of the trouble they're in. This disagreement gets them deeper into trouble. Their mutual attraction to each other makes the disagreement more intense.

The disagreement may be strong enough to cause the protagonist and contagonist to part ways (temporarily). Whether or not there is a physical separation, there will definitely be an emotional one.

If the antagonist is present, s/he may help or hinder either of the other two characters, and may do things to drive a wedge between them.

Whether the antagonist is present or not, s/he takes a step to solve his/her own story problem, which may affect the protagonist/contagonist now or in the future.

Brainstorming questions

In what ways to the protagonist and contagonist disagree on how to solve their new problem?

In what way is their mutual attraction intensifying their disagreement?

Do they stay together or part ways? And whichever happens, is it voluntary or involuntary?

How is the protagonist pressuring the contagonist to change his/her mind?

How is the contagonist pressuring the protagonist to change his/her mind?

Is the antagonist present? What is s/he doing right now?

After You Write

How many words did you write today?

How did it go?

Did you write at your scheduled time? If not, why not? When did you write instead? Why was this a better time?

Did you experience any distractions while you were writing?

How could you prevent those distractions from arising again? Or if they aren't avoidable, how could you minimize their impact on your writing in the future?

Did you experience any negative thoughts about writing at any time today?

Can you reframe those thoughts positively?

Day 12

Before You Write

The protagonist and/or contagonist escape from the frying pan
and into the fire. (If only one of them gets deeper into trouble,
this is still bad news for the other, who is going to have to
rescue them.)

The protagonist and/or the contagonist may have to
sacrifice something or take on an additional burden that
reduces their chances of success. This sacrifice makes the other
person respect the sacrificer more.

If the protagonist and/or the contagonist have parted ways,
they may regret it or be thankful that the other person has
escaped this new trouble. Either way, they should miss the
other in some way.

If the antagonist is present, s/he may help or hinder either
of the other two characters, and may do things to drive a wedge
between them.

Whether the antagonist is present or not, s/he takes a step to solve his/her own story problem, which may affect the protagonist/contagonist now or in the future.

Brainstorming questions

How do the attempts of the protagonist and contagonist to get out of trouble make things worse for them?

How do the protagonist and contagonist react to things getting even worse?

What does the protagonist and/or contagonist have to sacrifice to get them out of trouble?

If the protagonist and contagonist have been separated, how is each of them reacting to the separation?

If the protagonist and contagonist have been separated, what, if anything, are they doing to get back together again?

Is the antagonist present? What is s/he doing right now?

After You Write

How many words did you write today?

How did it go?

Did you write at your scheduled time? If not, why not? When did you write instead? Why was this a better time?

Did you experience any distractions while you were writing?

How could you prevent those distractions from arising again? Or if they aren't avoidable, how could you minimize their impact on your writing in the future?

Did you experience any negative thoughts about writing at any time today?

Can you reframe those thoughts positively?

Day 13

You are in the midst of a moving process. Nothing fails, then. All goes on. Work is done. If good, you learn from it. If bad, you learn even more.
  —Ray Bradbury

Before You Write

The protagonist and contagonist escape from their new problem. Doing so brings them back together again, if they parted earlier.

They may or may not admit/discuss/act on their attraction to each other, but they should both be feeling it more strongly than before.

Now that they are in a relatively safe place, they're forced to admit that they've got a long way to go.

Protagonist and contagonist come up with a new plan. One or both of them may be unhappy with this plan, but be unable to suggest a better one.

If the antagonist is present, s/he may help or hinder either of the other two characters, and may do things to drive a wedge between them.

Whether the antagonist is present or not, s/he takes a step

to solve his/her own story problem, which may affect the protagonist/contagonist now or in the future.

Brainstorming questions

How do the protagonist and contagonist escape from their newer, bigger problem?

How do they come back together again, if they do? How does each of them react to the reunion?

What new agreement do they come to regarding working together in the future?

How is their attraction to each other affecting their interaction?

What new plan do they come up with for achieving their goals?

Has either of them changed their ultimate goal in any way?

Is the antagonist present? What is s/he doing right now?

After You Write

How many words did you write today?

How did it go?

Did you write at your scheduled time? If not, why not? When did you write instead? Why was this a better time?

Did you experience any distractions while you were writing?

How could you prevent those distractions from arising again? Or if they aren't avoidable, how could you minimize their impact on your writing in the future?

Did you experience any negative thoughts about writing at any time today?

Can you reframe those thoughts positively?

Day 14

I want to stand as close to the edge as I can without going over. Out on the edge you see all the kinds of things you can't see from the center.
    —Kurt Vonnegut

Before You Write

The protagonist and contagonist begin to execute their new plan for solving their story problems. They may need to gather resources or allies first.

Their respective flaws make it even harder for them to work together, and they are disagreeing to an even greater degree than before. This disagreement may result in hurt feelings, prejudices and resentments being revealed, and/or one character learning something about the other that drives them apart emotionally.

If the antagonist is present, s/he may help or hinder either of the other two characters, and may do things to drive a wedge between them.

Whether the antagonist is present or not, s/he takes a step to solve his/her own story problem, which may affect the protagonist/contagonist now or in the future.

Brainstorming questions

What steps do the protagonist and contagonist take next?

How are their flaws making it harder to work together on this new plan?

What resources or allies do they need to gather in order for this plan to work?

What do they disagree about? How are their flaws (which serve as an internal antagonist) fueling this disagreement?

Whose feelings are hurt in this disagreement? What unpleasant truths are spoken? What painful secrets or hidden prejudices are revealed?

Is the antagonist present? What is s/he doing right now?

After You Write

How many words did you write today?

How did it go?

Did you write at your scheduled time? If not, why not? When did you write instead? Why was this a better time?

Did you experience any distractions while you were writing?

How could you prevent those distractions from arising again? Or if they aren't avoidable, how could you minimize their impact on your writing in the future?

Did you experience any negative thoughts about writing at any time today?

Can you reframe those thoughts positively?

Day 15

I think that when I get blocked, it's that I have something to say but I don't want to say it. So my mind says, "I have nothing to say." Closer to the truth is that I have a thought I really would prefer not to have.
—Paul Simon

Before You Write

The protagonist and contagonist continue to execute their new plan, which may involve gathering more resources, traveling to a new location, recruiting new allies, setting a trap, and/or collecting additional information.

Protagonist and/or contagonist may be smarting from their earlier disagreement and the hurtful things that were discussed. They may continue to fight, pointedly avoid fighting (or avoid conversation altogether), pretend that they are not upset, etc.

If the antagonist is present, s/he may help or hinder either of the other two characters, and may do things to drive a wedge between them.

Whether the antagonist is present or not, s/he takes a step to solve his/her own story problem, which may affect the protagonist/contagonist now or in the future. (You may or may not show it, but you should always know what your absent antagonist is up to.)

Brainstorming questions

What steps do the protagonist and contagonist take next?

In what ways are they still reacting to their hurt feelings?

In what ways are they failing to work together?

What efforts are they making, if any, to smooth things over?

Is the antagonist present? What is s/he doing right now?

After You Write

How many words did you write today?

How did it go?

Did you write at your scheduled time? If not, why not? When did you write instead? Why was this a better time?

Did you experience any distractions while you were writing?

How could you prevent those distractions from arising again? Or if they aren't avoidable, how could you minimize their impact on your writing in the future?

Did you experience any negative thoughts about writing at any time today?

Can you reframe those thoughts positively?

Day 16

You only fail if you stop writing.
   —Ray Bradbury

Before You Write

The protagonist and contagonist engage the antagonist's forces. At first, their plan seems to be working.

But the protagonist and/or contagonist lapses back into his/her old pattern, which makes executing the new plan a struggle and may create a new problem. They are forced to retreat/disengage from the conflict with the antagonist's forces.

If the antagonist is present, s/he may help or hinder either of the other two characters, and may do things to drive a wedge between them.

Whether the conflict results in a win, a lose, or a draw, the protagonist and contagonist are worse off in some way (loss of allies or resources, revealed weakness, antagonist strengthens his/her defenses, injuries, etc).

Whether the antagonist is present or not, s/he takes a step to solve his/her own story problem, which may affect the protagonist/contagonist now or in the future.

Brainstorming questions

How do the protagonist and contagonist engage the antagonist's forces?

In what way does their plan seem to be working?

In what way does the protagonist's and/or contagonist's flaw or wound keeping them from defeating the antagonist's forces?

What is the outcome of this encounter with the antagonist's forces?

How are the protagonist and contagonist worse off as a result of their encounter with the antagonist's forces?

How do the protagonist and contagonist react to the outcome of their encounter with the antagonist's forces?

How does the antagonist react? Is the antagonist present or is s/he working through minions?

How does this encounter affect the antagonist's plans?

After You Write

How many words did you write today?

How did it go?

Did you write at your scheduled time? If not, why not? When did you write instead? Why was this a better time?

Did you experience any distractions while you were writing?

How could you prevent those distractions from arising again? Or if they aren't avoidable, how could you minimize their impact on your writing in the future?

Did you experience any negative thoughts about writing at any time today?

Can you reframe those thoughts positively?

Day 17

Before You Write

Temporarily retreating from their conflict with the forces of the antagonist creates new problems for the protagonist and contagonist. The protagonist/contagonist react to their worsened position.

These new problems also bring their previous disagreement to a head, but gives them an opportunity to resolve one aspect of their romantic conflict (not the entire conflict). Apologies may be made or traded, and amends may be made for the hurt inflicted.

If the antagonist is present, s/he may help or hinder either of the other two characters, and may do things to drive a wedge between them.

Whether the antagonist is present or not, s/he takes a step to solve his/her own story problem, which may affect the protagonist/contagonist now or in the future.

Brainstorming questions

What new problems are created as a result of the protagonist's and contagonist's defeat (or victory with unexpected negative consequences)?

How do these new problems trigger the protagonist and contagonist to fight?

What aspect of the romantic conflict do the protagonist and contagonist resolve as they try to hash out their disagreement about how to defeat the villain? Does one of them (or both) apologize? Or make a peace offering? Or admit that the other was right?

What new plan do the protagonist and contagonist come up with for achieving their respective goals?

Has the protagonist's and/or contagonist's goals changed or shifted in any way as a result of their recent defeat?

Is the antagonist present? What is s/he doing right now?

After You Write

How many words did you write today?

How did it go?

Did you write at your scheduled time? If not, why not? When did you write instead? Why was this a better time?

Did you experience any distractions while you were writing?

How could you prevent those distractions from arising again? Or if they aren't avoidable, how could you minimize their impact on your writing in the future?

Did you experience any negative thoughts about writing at any time today?

Can you reframe those thoughts positively?

Day 18

So many of our dreams at first seem impossible, then they seem improbable, and then, when we summon the will they become inevitable.
—Christopher Reeve

Before You Write

The protagonist and contagonist begin to execute their new plan, which turns out to be harder than expected. They may switch directions, redeploy resources in a new way, or attack with renewed vigor. In spite of their struggles, they're making progress.

Now that protagonist and contagonist have made amends for their earlier fighting, their attraction gets stronger. They may act on it or spend more energy resisting it.

The protagonist and contagonist each reflect on how his/her flaw caused trouble during their last conflict with the antagonist's forces and resolves to overcome it for good. (Since you will be in one of these characters' POV, you will need to show through dialogue or actions that the non-POV character has made a mental shift, rather than showing the realization directly.)

If the antagonist is present, s/he may help or hinder either of the other two characters, and may do things to drive a wedge between them.

Whether the antagonist is present or not, s/he takes a step to solve his/her own story problem, which may affect the protagonist/contagonist now or in the future.

Brainstorming questions

What is the next step the protagonist and contagonist take? Why does it turn out to be harder than expected?

In what ways does their stronger attraction to each other manifest? Are they resisting it or giving in to it?

How is their attraction to each other making it harder for them to execute their new plan?

How has the protagonist's and/or contagonist's thinking about their respective flaws changed? What strengthens their resolve to overcome their flaws/wounds?

Is the antagonist present? What is s/he doing right now?

After You Write

How many words did you write today?

How did it go?

Did you write at your scheduled time? If not, why not? When did you write instead? Why was this a better time?

Did you experience any distractions while you were writing?

How could you prevent those distractions from arising again? Or if they aren't avoidable, how could you minimize their impact on your writing in the future?

Did you experience any negative thoughts about writing at any time today?

Can you reframe those thoughts positively?

Day 19

I think the less attention I pay to what people want and the more I pay to just writing the book I want to write, the better I do.
—Lawrence Block

Before You Write

The protagonist and contagonist continue to make progress with their plan, although they uncover a new problem that causes them to worry that their plan will not be good enough to defeat the antagonist.

Depending on how their relationship has progressed, they may or may not fight about what to do. But this disagreement doesn't dampen their newly-strengthened relationship: they're getting the hang of working together.

The protagonist and/or contagonist seems to be doing well at overcoming his/her flaw.

If the antagonist is present, s/he may help or hinder either of the other two characters, and may do things to drive a wedge between them. Whether the antagonist is present or not, s/he takes a step to solve his/her own story problem, which may affect the protagonist/contagonist now or in the future.

Brainstorming questions

What progress are the protagonist and contagonist making?

What new problems are they encountering as they execute their plan to defeat the antagonist? What worries are these problems triggering?

In what ways do the protagonist and contagonist still disagree? In what ways is each winning the other over?

In what ways is the protagonist and/or contagonist resisting the urge to fall back into his/her flaw or to be controlled by his/her flaw or wound?

Is the antagonist present? What is s/he doing right now?

After You Write

How many words did you write today?

How did it go?

Did you write at your scheduled time? If not, why not? When did you write instead? Why was this a better time?

Did you experience any distractions while you were writing?

How could you prevent those distractions from arising again? Or if they aren't avoidable, how could you minimize their impact on your writing in the future?

Did you experience any negative thoughts about writing at any time today?

Can you reframe those thoughts positively?

Day 20

Talent is cheaper than table salt. What separates the talented individual from the successful one is a lot of hard work.
—Stephen King

Before You Write

The protagonist and contagonist seem close to defeating the antagonist's forces, but something unexpected stops them before they can complete their plan. It's possible that one of them deviates from the plan in order to protect the other from an unexpected problem.

This new setback puts a strain on their newly-strengthened relationship. As the plan falls through, the characters' feelings for each other intensifies and they may disagree on what should happen next.

If the antagonist is present, s/he may help or hinder either of the other two characters, and may do things to drive a wedge between them.

Whether the antagonist is present or not, s/he takes a step to solve his/her own story problem, which may affect the protagonist/contagonist now or in the future.

Brainstorming questions

In what ways does it seem that the protagonist and contagonist are close to defeating the antagonist's forces?

What unexpected twist stops them from completing their plan?

How do the protagonist and/or contagonist deal with this unexpected twist?

How does this new problem put a new strain on their relationship?

Is the antagonist present? What is s/he doing right now?

After You Write

How many words did you write today?

How did it go?

Did you write at your scheduled time? If not, why not? When did you write instead? Why was this a better time?

Did you experience any distractions while you were writing?

How could you prevent those distractions from arising again? Or if they aren't avoidable, how could you minimize their impact on your writing in the future?

Did you experience any negative thoughts about writing at any time today?

Can you reframe those thoughts positively?

Day 21

It's better to write about things you feel than about things you know about.
      —L P. Hartley

Before You Write

The protagonist and contagonist continue their conflict with the antagonist's forces. Victory no longer seems certain. They are likely to try something desperate.

Either the protagonist or the contagonist may slip under pressure and make a mistake that helps the antagonist. This mistake makes it clear that even though they're trying to work together, they're still learning to be a team and they still haven't resolved their fundamental romantic conflict.

The protagonist's and/or contagonist's flaw may resurface at a crucial moment.

If the antagonist is present, s/he may help or hinder either of the other two characters, and may do things to drive a wedge between them.

Whether the antagonist is present or not, s/he takes a step to solve his/her own story problem, which may affect the protagonist/contagonist now or in the future.

Brainstorming questions

What desperate thing(s) do the protagonist and/or contagonist attempt in order to defeat the antagonist's forces?

What mistakes do they make in their desperation?

How does their teamwork fail at a crucial moment?

What aspect of the romantic conflict do they still need to solve?

How does the protagonist's and/or contagonist's flaw affect this crucial moment?

Is the antagonist present, or are the protagonist/contagonist dealing with minions? What is the antagonist doing right now?

After You Write

How many words did you write today?

How did it go?

Did you write at your scheduled time? If not, why not? When did you write instead? Why was this a better time?

Did you experience any distractions while you were writing?

How could you prevent those distractions from arising again? Or if they aren't avoidable, how could you minimize their impact on your writing in the future?

Did you experience any negative thoughts about writing at any time today?

Can you reframe those thoughts positively?

Day 22

The basic difference between an ordinary man and a warrior is that a warrior takes everything as a challenge, while an ordinary man takes everything either as a blessing or a curse.
   —Carlos Castaneda

Before You Write

Protagonist and contagonist experience their biggest defeat so far. They may withdraw or be captured.

This defeat creates new doubts about the future of their relationship.

If the antagonist is present, s/he may help or hinder either of the other two characters, and may do things to drive a wedge between them.

Whether the antagonist is present or not, s/he takes a step to solve his/her own story problem, which may affect the protagonist/contagonist now or in the future.

Brainstorming questions

How do the protagonist and contagonist react to their biggest defeat so far? How do their respective flaws/wounds affect their reactions?

What kind of trouble are they in now?

What doubts does this situation create about the future of their relationship?

What have the protagonist and contagonist lost as a result of this defeat, both personally and in terms of their relationship?

Is the antagonist present? What is s/he doing right now?

After You Write

How many words did you write today?

How did it go?

Did you write at your scheduled time? If not, why not? When did you write instead? Why was this a better time?

Did you experience any distractions while you were writing?

How could you prevent those distractions from arising again? Or if they aren't avoidable, how could you minimize their impact on your writing in the future?

Did you experience any negative thoughts about writing at any time today?

Can you reframe those thoughts positively?

Day 23

The harder I work, the luckier I get.
   —Samuel Goldwyn

Before You Write

This is the dark moment, where the protagonist and/or contagonist momentarily loses faith in him/herself and his/her mission.

They may or may not offer each other comfort and/or advice, depending on the state of their relationship here. They may argue from their doubts. One or both of them may temporarily give up on their story goal.

These doubts maybe bleed into the relationship and intensify the romantic conflict, or they may bring the protagonist and contagonist closer together (but at the same time, make the future they were hoping for seem impossible).

The protagonist and contagonist may part ways. Even if they stay together, they must grapple with their new doubts about their relationship.

If the antagonist is present, s/he may help or hinder either of the other two characters, and may do things to drive a wedge between them.

Whether the antagonist is present or not, s/he takes a step to solve his/her own story problem, which may affect the protagonist/contagonist now or in the future.

Brainstorming questions

What is the trigger for the protagonist and/or the contagonist losing faith?

What comfort or advice do they give/receive, if any?

Do they stay together, or do they separate?

What new doubts about their relationship are raised as a result of this loss of faith?

Is the antagonist present? What is s/he doing right now?

After You Write

How many words did you write today?

How did it go?

Did you write at your scheduled time? If not, why not? When did you write instead? Why was this a better time?

Did you experience any distractions while you were writing?

How could you prevent those distractions from arising again? Or if they aren't avoidable, how could you minimize their impact on your writing in the future?

Did you experience any negative thoughts about writing at any time today?

Can you reframe those thoughts positively?

Day 24

Those who write are writers. Those who wait are waiters.
　　—A. Lee Martinez

Before You Write

The protagonist and contagonist regain their faith; it is likely that one of them finds a new reason to hope first and then convinces the other that all is not lost.

If they have separated, the one who regains hope first goes looking for the other.

They commit to defeating the antagonist's forces no matter what, and come up with a new plan. If the contagonist is present, s/he may help with the plan.

They are still grappling with their doubts about the future of this relationship, but one or both of them has discovered a sliver of hope that the relationship has a future.

If the antagonist is present, s/he may help or hinder either of the other two characters, and may do things to drive a wedge between them. Whether the antagonist is present or not, s/he takes a step to solve his/her own story problem, which may affect the protagonist/contagonist now or in the future.

Brainstorming questions

What experience(s) cause the protagonist and/or contagonist to regain their faith and recommit to defeating the antagonist?

If they are together, how do they help each other with this? If they are not together, which one seeks out the other, and what is necessary to convince the other to rejoin the quest?

What is their new plan for defeating the antagonist?

What experience or realization causes the protagonist and/or contagonist to discover a sliver of hope that their relationship has a future?

Do they talk about this sliver of hope, or do they keep it to themselves?

Is the antagonist present? What is s/he doing right now?

After You Write

How many words did you write today?

How did it go?

Did you write at your scheduled time? If not, why not? When did you write instead? Why was this a better time?

Did you experience any distractions while you were writing?

How could you prevent those distractions from arising again? Or if they aren't avoidable, how could you minimize their impact on your writing in the future?

Did you experience any negative thoughts about writing at any time today?

Can you reframe those thoughts positively?

Day 25

Before You Write

The protagonist and contagonist gather allies and resources as needed, and perform whatever tasks are needed to set up their attack on the antagonist's forces.

Their hopes for their relationship's future and the fear of being disappointed are both raised.

If the antagonist is present, s/he may help or hinder either of the other two characters, and may do things to drive a wedge between them.

Whether the antagonist is present or not, s/he takes a step to solve his/her own story problem, which may affect the protagonist/contagonist now or in the future.

Brainstorming questions

What allies and resources do the protagonist and contagonist gather? What tasks do they need to accomplish to set their plan in action?

What obstacles do they overcome as they gather resources/allies and prepare for the final confrontation?

What experience(s) and realization(s) cause their hopes and fears to be raised?

Is the antagonist present? What is s/he doing right now?

After You Write

How many words did you write today?

How did it go?

Did you write at your scheduled time? If not, why not? When did you write instead? Why was this a better time?

Did you experience any distractions while you were writing?

How could you prevent those distractions from arising again? Or if they aren't avoidable, how could you minimize their impact on your writing in the future?

Did you experience any negative thoughts about writing at any time today?

Can you reframe those thoughts positively?

Day 26

There's no right way of writing. There's only your way.
  —Milton Lomask

Before You Write

The protagonist, contagonist, and other allies begin their attack on the antagonist's forces. It should be an uphill battle, even if the fight is not a physical one.

Their hopes of being together are further raised, as is their fear of discovering that their relationship has no future.

If the antagonist is present, s/he may help or hinder either of the other two characters, and may do things to drive a wedge between them.

Whether the antagonist is present or not, s/he takes a step to solve his/her own story problem, which may affect the protagonist/contagonist now or in the future.

Brainstorming questions

How do the protagonist, contagonist and their allies attack the antagonist's forces?

How do the protagonist and contagonist react to the obstacles they encounter?

How do the protagonist and contagonist overcome these obstacles?

How does overcoming these obstacles strengthen the love between protagonist and contagonist?

What experience(s) and realization(s) further raise their hopes and increase their fears?

Is the antagonist present? What is s/he doing right now?

After You Write

How many words did you write today?

How did it go?

Did you write at your scheduled time? If not, why not? When did you write instead? Why was this a better time?

Did you experience any distractions while you were writing?

How could you prevent those distractions from arising again? Or if they aren't avoidable, how could you minimize their impact on your writing in the future?

Did you experience any negative thoughts about writing at any time today?

Can you reframe those thoughts positively?

Day 27

In quickness is truth. The more swiftly you write, the more honest you are. In hesitation is thought. In delay comes the effort for a style, instead of leaping upon truth which is the only style worth deadfalling or tiger-trapping.
—Ray Bradbury

Before You Write

The protagonist, contagonist, and other allies fight the antagonist's forces. (Usually, they will have to go through any minions first before they get access to the antagonist.)

Their hope for the future of the relationship becomes hope for the survival of the other person, and their fear for the future of the relationship becomes fear of losing the other person.

If the antagonist is present, s/he may help or hinder either of the other two characters, and may do things to drive a wedge between them.

Whether the antagonist is present or not, s/he takes a step to solve his/her own story problem, which may affect the protagonist/contagonist now or in the future.

Brainstorming questions

How does the fight change as the protagonist's forces get closer to the antagonist?

What new obstacles threaten the very survival of the protagonist and/or contagonist?

How do the protagonist and contagonist react to the new, heightened threats to each other's survival?

Is the antagonist present? What is s/he doing right now?

After You Write

How many words did you write today?

How did it go?

Did you write at your scheduled time? If not, why not? When did you write instead? Why was this a better time?

Did you experience any distractions while you were writing?

How could you prevent those distractions from arising again? Or if they aren't avoidable, how could you minimize their impact on your writing in the future?

Did you experience any negative thoughts about writing at any time today?

Can you reframe those thoughts positively?

Day 28

Before You Write

The protagonist is separated from the contagonist and other allies by the antagonist's forces. The contagonist may be threatened by the antagonist, and is likely in the antagonist's power. The other allies may die, be captured or disabled, be driven off, or even be coopted by the antagonist's forces.

The separation of the protagonist and contagonist (even if it is just bars in adjacent jail cells) forces them to face the possibility of life without each other. They no longer doubt their feelings, but it looks like the antagonist is going to destroy their relationship and/or deprive them of the future they want to build together.

If the antagonist is present, s/he may help or hinder either of the other two characters, and may do things to drive a wedge between them. Whether the antagonist is present or not, s/he takes a step to solve his/her own story problem, which may affect the protagonist/contagonist now or in the future.

Brainstorming questions

How are the protagonist and contagonist separated from their allies, and then from each other?

What is their reaction to being separated from their allies?

What is their reaction to being separated from each other?

What triggers the belief in the protagonist that the contagonist is right for him/her?

What triggers the belief in the contagonist that the protagonist is right for him/her?

How do the protagonist and/or contagonist react to the realization that if they had recognized their love sooner, things might have turned out differently? What do they wish they had said or not said? How would they do things differently if they had a second chance?

Is the antagonist present? What is s/he doing right now?

After You Write

How many words did you write today?

How did it go?

Did you write at your scheduled time? If not, why not? When did you write instead? Why was this a better time?

Did you experience any distractions while you were writing?

How could you prevent those distractions from arising again? Or if they aren't avoidable, how could you minimize their impact on your writing in the future?

Did you experience any negative thoughts about writing at any time today?

Can you reframe those thoughts positively?

Day 29

You are always naked when you start writing; you are always as if you had never written anything before; you are always a beginner. Shakespeare wrote without knowing he would become Shakespeare.
—Erica Jong

Before You Write

The protagonist and contagonist battle the antagonist, either serially or simultaneously. The antagonist tries to use the protagonist's and contagonist's flaws against them.

Both protagonist and contagonist are willing to sacrifice themselves to save the other. Their love for each other gives them the strength to defeat the antagonist together.

The protagonist/contagonist win, either by overcoming their flaws or finding a way to turn those flaws into strengths. Whichever path they choose, the antagonist is defeated through his own flaw.

The major conflict of the story is resolved and the story's main question is answered (or if this is an ongoing series, progress is made toward answering it).

Brainstorming questions

How do the protagonist and contagonist battle the antagonist?

How does the antagonist try to use their flaws against them? Why doesn't it work?

In what ways do the protagonist and/or contagonist sacrifice themselves for each other?

In what ways do the protagonist and/or contagonist demonstrate that they have overcome their flaws?

How do the protagonist and contagonist work together to defeat the antagonist?

How do the protagonist and/or contagonist use the antagonist's flaw against him/her?

What mistake does the antagonist make that results in his/her defeat?

After You Write

How many words did you write today?

How did it go?

Did you write at your scheduled time? If not, why not? When did you write instead? Why was this a better time?

Did you experience any distractions while you were writing?

How could you prevent those distractions from arising again? Or if they aren't avoidable, how could you minimize their impact on your writing in the future?

Did you experience any negative thoughts about writing at any time today?

Can you reframe those thoughts positively?

Day 30

> *You never know what's around the corner. It could*
> *be everything. Or it could be nothing. You keep*
> *putting one foot in front of the other, and then one*
> *day you look back and you've climbed a mountain.*
> —Tom Hiddleston

Before You Write

Today, you'll tie up all the loose ends: show the reader the fallout from the battle between protagonist and antagonist, and how everyone involved is affected.

The protagonist and contagonist either return to their ordinary world changed people or they make a new home in the extraordinary world.

You'll also show the protagonist and contagonist affirming their love for each other and hint at their happy future together.

Brainstorming questions

What emotion will you end the story on? How do you want your reader to feel when they close this book?

How does the battle between protagonist and antagonist change their lives, and the lives of everyone around them?

What happens to the antagonist? Is s/he dead, exiled, shamed into submission or jailed? Is s/he redeemed?

What do the protagonist and contagonist gain as a result of defeating the antagonist? What do they lose?

What loose ends need to be tied up?

How do the protagonist and contagonist express their love for each other?

What kind of future will the protagonist and contagonist have together?

After You Write

How many words did you write today?

How did it go?

Did you write at your scheduled time? If not, why not? When did you write instead? Why was this a better time?

Did you experience any distractions while you were writing?

How could you prevent those distractions from arising again? Or if they aren't avoidable, how could you minimize their impact on your writing in the future?

Did you experience any negative thoughts about writing at any time today?

Can you reframe those thoughts positively?

Congratulations!

Time to celebrate your creativity and your persistence! Give yourself a pat on the back, do a victory dance, and claim that big reward you promised yourself back when you started this writing marathon.

You won.

You finished a novel.

You're a novelist.

Let that sink in for a minute, especially if this is your first one.

So many people say they're going to write a novel someday, but few start writing—and even fewer finish. No matter what happens after this, you've proven that you've got what it takes to be a writer.

What If I Didn't Finish?

Let's start by figuring out why you didn't finish your novel.

Were you not able to hit your daily word count goal?

That's not uncommon. It sounds good to say "I'm going to write 2,000 words every day for 30 days," but that's easier said than done.

How many words *were* you able to write each day? Do you know your hourly average? If you've set aside 2 hours each day to write and you're able to write 500 words each hour, that means you're going to either need to set aside more time or you're going to need more than 30 days.

Don't despair. Writing is a habit, and the more you write, the more you will be able to write.

Set your daily word count slightly higher than you're managing right now, and as soon as that starts to feel easy, set it a little higher. Yes, that means it might take 45, 60, maybe even 90 days for you to finish your novel. But you're still way ahead of those who take years to write a novel.

If 30 days of writing left you feeling exhausted or burned out, I recommend taking a couple of weeks or perhaps even a month off before you start another writing marathon. Or set the daily goal even lower and give yourself a few months to finish at a pace that isn't so tiring.

Did you get stuck in some part of the story?

This happens a lot too—maybe you're a newer writer who's still developing their bag of tricks for dealing with thorny story problems, or maybe you're a more advanced writer who's tackling a very challenging type of story.

If the tips in *What If I Get Stuck* don't help, you might want to:

- Find someone to brainstorm with—if you're already not in a writing group with others who are writing similar types of stories, look for one online. Bouncing ideas off another writer and talking through the logic of your story is one of the fastest ways to get a new perspective and generate new ideas.
- Read a book on how to plot (there's a recommended list in *How to Use This Journal*) and use the exercises in it to figure out what should happen next.
- Find a critique partner, preferably someone who reads in your genre, even if they're not writing in it. It's much easier to see clearly what's wrong with a story when you're not the one writing it.

Was it too hard to stick to your writing schedule?

Life does get in the way sometimes, and if you've had a major disruption during your 30 days, like a family member falling ill or an unexpected crisis at work, you probably had to set the novel aside for a bit to deal with it. It happens to all of us.

Once you've dealt with the crisis, come back to your draft and figure out how many days you'll need to finish. Schedule those writing days on your calendar, and give yourself a new finish date to shoot for.

But maybe the problem wasn't a major disruption—maybe your schedule wasn't realistic enough, and you need to set a slower pace to account for the fact that your kids need lunches and rides to soccer practice and bedtime stories. An easier schedule with a slightly longer writing period—say, 60 days—might be what you need to get back on track.

For those of you who aren't sure why you had trouble sticking to your writing schedule, I encourage you to think for a few moments on what you did when you were supposed to be writing. Were you vegging out in front of the TV or playing video games or chatting with your BFF online?

If you've fallen prey to procrastination in the form of mindless recreation, it's possible that you're not taking good enough care of yourself physically. Vegging out is often a response to feeling tired and burned out—your energy levels are low and you're looking for something to do while you recuperate.

The frustrating thing about this type of mindless recreation is that it's often not energizing, because while you're watching TV or surfing Facebook, there's a voice back in your head nagging you about the writing (and other things) you're supposed to be doing.

If you think this is your problem, I have two suggestions:

First, see if there's something else you could do to raise your physical energy levels. Do you need to drink more water, eat more veggies, or go for more walks? Are you only getting five hours of sleep a night? Could you use a little quiet time every morning or evening?

Second, when you feel like doing something mindless, choose to do something that will actually give you more energy. Take a nap. Go for a walk. Put on some happy music and dance. Pace or do some deep breathing while you watch *one* episode of a beloved TV show. After you've done something energizing, sit down and use some of that energy to write one sentence. Just one.

(Okay, you can write more than one if you feel like it.)

If you get into the habit of taking better care of yourself so your energy levels are higher, and then you use a small portion of that extra energy to work on your novel, you'll build a sustainable writing habit that will gain momentum over time, until you're unstoppable.

Was your story too big to tell in 30 days?

Even for pros, writing 90,000 words in 30 days is a big push. If you're writing an epic that's even longer than this, it might not be possible for you to finish it in 30 days. And you might not realize how big the story is until you start writing.

If that's the case, look at how many words you've written, and where you are in the story. Did it take you 40,000 words to get to the end of Act One (the scene where the protagonist entered his/her extraordinary world)? Act One is usually about one-quarter of the story. That means you'd be reasonable to estimate that the whole story is going to take 160,000 words to tell.

If you discover you're writing such an epic, you can use your average daily word count to figure out how many days it will realistically take you to finish.

Then, unless you're planning to self-publish, ask yourself if there's some way you might break the story down into two or three books (80,000 to 120,000 words each). Because when a book runs longer than 100,000 words, the printing costs cuts into the publisher's profit margin so much that they're more nervous about investing in it.

Celebrating The Progress You *Did* Make

I recommend that, no matter how much you write, you celebrate the part of your story that you did write during your 30 day writing marathon.

Starting a novel is an accomplishment. Most people who say they'd like to write a novel someday never manage to write the first sentence. Celebrate getting your foot in the door. Then make a plan for how you're going to write the rest.

If you filled out even a few of the daily entries, you probably learned something about what stops you from writing and what you need to write. Celebrate learning more about your creative process. Then use that information to figure out how you'll do things differently so that it's easier to overcome your writing obstacles.

If you got swamped by a life emergency and didn't get started...it happens. We can't put our lives on hold to write a novel, even though sometimes we might wish we could. But if you're reading this paragraph, you haven't give up yet on your dream of writing a novel. Take care of the emergency and any loved ones who are affected by it.

When you can breathe again, celebrate that dream of being a novelist that you've been nurturing deep inside. Then open your calendar and choose the day you're going to start writing that novel.

Editing Your Novel

Creativity is allowing yourself to make mistakes.
Art is knowing which ones to keep.
  —Scott Adams

Now that you've finished the rough draft, the next step is editing.

I recommend setting your novel aside for a couple of weeks or more before you edit anything.

Why?

First, because you've just pushed your mind and body through a grueling 30-day journey. Before you make any more important decisions about your story, you need to give yourself a chance to recuperate.

Second, because you're still emotionally invested in your story. Editing requires that you look at what you've written with a dispassionate eye. You need to get some distance from your novel before you start making decisions about what to keep and what to change.

I also recommend that you resist the urge to hand out copies to your friends and family to read, at least for now. Even the people who love you most won't be able to resist making one little comment about that one scene that needs a lot of work, and because you're still so close to the story, you're probably going to feel defensive.

Or furious.

Or utterly depressed.

Don't do that to yourself.

Instead, invite your loved ones to celebrate with you, tell them what the novel's about (briefly) if they ask, and let them know you'll be mentioning them in the acknowledgements.

But if they ask to read it, smile mysteriously and tell them not yet. You still need to edit it.

What If I Don't Know Know to Edit a Novel?

After I wrote my first novel, I waited a week before I opened the file, thinking that I would fix a few grammatical problems, maybe embellish some descriptions.

But about ten pages into my edit, I felt like I'd been sucker-punched.

My characters weren't as amazing as they'd seemed in my head. The story was unfolding more slowly than I remembered. My dialogue was wooden and my setting descriptions were awful.

I was so overwhelmed at the prospect of fixing it, I almost gave up.

These days, when I edit a novel, I have a structured process that allows me to focus on one thing at a time and identify all the necessary changes before I fix anything.

First, I read the story through once as if I'm a reader and jot down my general impressions. I don't try to figure out how to fix anything—I just note where the story drags, where the characters' personalities aren't coming through strongly enough, etc. (You can jot notes directly on the page or you can make a chapter-by-chapter list.)

Once I've done this first read-through, I take a week to mull these problems over.

Then I get out the colored pens and I read it again, **focusing just on the story.**

- Does each thing that happens make sense?
- Are the events causally-linked? In other words, are later events caused by earlier events in the story?
- Do the characters act out-of-character, and if so, how? Do they stop trying to reach their goals or behave illogically at any place in the story?
- Have I explained everything to the reader that s/he needs to know to get the story?
- Are there are any scenes that feel rushed or boringly slow? Any scenes that don't focus on an interesting and meaningful conflict?
- Is the setting of each scene described well enough for the reader to imagine where the characters are?

Each time I find a problem, I stop reading and brainstorm ways that I might fix it. I don't just stop at the first solution, because often the fourth or fifth idea is better.

Once I've read the whole novel a second time and come up with possible solutions to my story problems, I decide which solutions I'm going to use and I check each one off as I rewrite.

Only after the story problems are fixed do I worry about making the dialogue better or making sure character emotions are coming through clearly or polishing each sentence.

Learning How to Edit

If you want to improve your editing skills, here are some resources:

Editing for Emotion: Hands-On Techniques for Creating Emotional Impact (Lynn Johnston)

This workshop teaches my own personal system for taking a lackluster manuscript and maximizing its emotional impact on the reader.

If you're getting feedback from your readers that your characters are one-dimensional, that you're telling too much and not showing enough, or that your story didn't grab them and they can't explain why, this in-depth workshop can show you how to bring your story to life.

Available at: www.writesmarternotharder.com/courses/

One-Pass Manuscript Revision: From First Draft to Last in One Cycle (Holly Lisle)

Holly is one of my favorite writing teachers, and every single workshop and book she's written is fantastic. This free article teaches her one-pass revision method—a highly-organized approach to fixing your novel's story problems.

If you try her process and start to feel overwhelmed, I recommend giving yourself permission to do more than one pass, and break her checklist down into sections.

Available at: http://hollylisle.com/one-pass-manuscript-revision-from-first-draft-to-last-in-one-cycle/

How To Revise Your Novel: Get the Book You WANT From the Wreck You Wrote (Holly Lisle)

If you can afford Holly's multi-month revision workshop, I recommend it highly. She'll teach you numerous techniques for discovering and fixing the flaws in your novel, and you'll come away from it a much stronger writer.

Available at: https://howtothinksideways.com/shop/how-to-revise-your-novel/

Rock Your Revisions: A Simple System for Revising Your Novel (Cathy Yardley)

The best thing about Cathy's approach to revision is that she's brilliant at explaining novel structure in clear, simple terms that will help you tell your story in the best possible way. If terms like "three act structure," "plot points," and "pinch points" are unfamiliar to you, you need to read this inexpensive ebook.

Available at: http://www.amazon.com/Rock-Your-Revisions-Revising-Writing-ebook/dp/B00AFB653K/

Author's Note

I hope you found this workbook helpful, and wish you the best with your writing.

For more resources to help you succeed as a writer, visit my website: www.writesmarternotharder.com

If you'd like to ask me a question or let me know how your 30-day writing marathon went, you can contact me at: kaizenlynn@gmail.com

Happy writing!

Lynn

P.S. If you enjoyed this book, would you please leave a review and help others discover it?

Editing for Emotion

Hands-On Techniques for Creating Emotional Impact

You started out with a great premise, larger-than-life characters, and a fast-paced plot. Your walls are plastered with goal-motivation-conflict charts and you could recite each character's internal and external arcs in your sleep. Maybe you even came up with a detailed outline before you started writing your latest masterpiece.

But now that it's time to edit your rough draft, you realize your characters' emotions and personalities didn't make it onto the page, and the scenes that were so vivid in your head seem flat or rushed on paper. What went wrong?

Nothing, actually. First drafts are for getting the basic story nailed down. Revision is where you crank up the voltage and get the emotions right.

This workshop focuses on practical techniques to help you edit the spark back into your story. Topics covered include:

- Why stimulus-response chains can make or break a scene, and how to use them for maximum dramatic effect
- How to fine-tune the progression of emotion in a scene
- Techniques for infusing the POV character's personality and worldview into each scene
- How to streamline exposition and make infodumps do double-duty as characterization
- Why descriptions are inherently boring, and how you can make them compelling
- How to write narrative summary that your readers won't

be tempted to skim
- How to recognize and eliminate author intrusion
- How to make sure your characters' emotions make it onto the page

At the end of the workshop, you'll have an editing checklist that guides you through the process of transforming your rough draft into the exciting, dynamic story you originally envisioned.

Register at: www.writesmarternotharder.com/courses/

What Students Are Saying About
Edit the Life Back Into Your Novel

Lynn has a way of nurturing fledgling authors into powerful storytellers. As a direct result of her class I'm now a published author with a New York editor who consistently seeks out my work.

—Paula Millhouse, author of *Dragonstone*

This workshop changed my life. Editing has always been the hardest part of writing for me. Lynn gives you a plan which breaks the process down into manageable, bite size pieces.

Her detailed and incredibly perceptive feedback is by far the most valuable part of the course. She is the most superb teacher I've ever had the pleasure of learning from.

—Samantha MacDouglas

This workshop really opened my eyes and made my writing so much better! The best part was the feedback I was given on my own project. I would have gladly paid ten times what I did for this class; it was worth every penny.

—Stacy McKitrick, author of *My Sunny Vampire*

I believe Lynn's class is the reason I'm a finalist in two RWA contests this year. This workshop and Lynn's devotion to detail will bring out the best in your story and you.

—Elizabeth W. Gibson

This workshop fundamentally improved my writing.

Lynn's lessons are easy to understand but challenging to complete, guiding you toward a deeper understanding of what makes a story work.

Lynn appreciates that every writer uses a different process. She supports, and can help you improve, your writing style, from pantser to plotter and everything in between.

If you want your story to pop off the page and into the imagination of readers, don't waste your money on any other course, just take this one.

—Kayle Allen

The quality and depth of my writing improved dramatically when I took *Edit the Life Back Into Your Story*.

She taught me how to break down a scene so that instead of simply depicting a series of events, I now incorporate character reactions (emotions, thoughts, inner monologue) to each of those events.

Lynn's classes are hard—she demands a lot from her students—but you walk away with the knowledge and skill to write much better stories.

—Pauline Gruber, author of *The Girl and the Raven*

The Writer's Guide to Getting Organized

Take Control of Your Creative Life 10 Minutes at a Time

Writers are different. We don't always think in straight lines. We take leaps of logic, we think metaphorically, and we know in order to make something beautiful, you might also have to make a mess.

You've probably tried to adopt at least one organizing system already. Maybe it was in a bestselling book written by someone in a suit. Or maybe it was the system that works for your brother the accountant or your naturally-neat coworker. Whatever system you tried, it was probably very logical and made total sense, until you tried to force yourself to fit into it.

Did you come to the conclusion that there's something wrong with you? That you're naturally disorganized? That creativity and organization can't coexist?

First the good news: you're not broken, and it is possible to be creative and organized at the same time.

Any functional system of organization for writers must be designed around the writing process. And every writer's process is a little bit different.

This book will show you how to analyze your writing process and set up your tools and resources in a way that feels natural and supports you in being more creatively successful.

A lifesaver for creatives who struggle to get and stay organized!

Available at: http://www.amazon.com/The-Writers-Guide-Getting-Organized-ebook/dp/B005ZGXCV8/

Made in the USA
San Bernardino, CA
03 August 2017